SIBLING SAPLINGS

Anne Frank's Diary Lives Through
Horse Chestnut Trees

by Mary Kay Worth

Ordering Information:

You may search this book in Amazon, Barnes & Nobles and other online retailers by searching using the ISBN below.

ISBN (eBook): 978-1-961225-63-3
ISBN (Paperback): 978-1-961225-64-0
ISBN (Hardback): 978-1-961225-65-7

CONTENTS

DEDICATION

Bill Zimpher has been involved in this project since the very beginning. A middle school English teacher at Southern Cayuga Central School, Aurora, NY, Bill came to me to ask for support as the Superintendent of Schools in the summer of 2009. The grant proposed was to be one of the recipients of a tree seedling. This seedling was from the DNA of the Horse Chestnut tree that Anne Frank wrote about in her famous diary. In hiding, the Jewish girl peeked out of the attic window in Amsterdam. It became a sign of hope that Anne wrote about.

Bill wrote the grant. Eleven original seedings were awarded. SCCS was named as a recipient. Later, in 2019, Bill was named as the New York State Teacher of the Year specifically for his role in continuing education focused on tolerance and acceptance of differences. I was in Albany, NY, for the honor.

Bill has provided guidance throughout the writing of *Sibling Saplings*. At this printing, Bill still teaches at SCCS. He is a colleague and friend. The dedication couldn't be more appropriate.

ABOUT THE AUTHOR

Child of God, Grandma, Mother, Daughter, Sister, Friend
Person with Disabilities
Teacher, Principal, Superintendent, Professor
Traveler, Storyteller, Photographer, Actor, Musician,
Author, Owner

Mary Kay is a native of Portville, NY, and now lives in Lakeland, FL. Following 30+ years in public education, Mary Kay has ten titles: *HEY ELEPHANT! WHERE ARE YOU?* , *Banele – the Girl from Swaziland, Mountains Trees Plant and Flowers of Swaziland, Dear Deer, The Truth About Santa, Three Christmas Stories, Pop Pop's Train Ride, The Great Train Robbery, A Lucky Stone Day,* and *Sibling Saplings.*

Good River Print and Media has republished and illustrated 5 books and books #9 and #10.

Available through Mary Kay's website or Amazon.
For more information check out Mary Kay's website:
http://www.marykayworthofficial.com .

Chapter 1

I will find them all. We arrived together. There were 11 of us.

I WILL FIND THEM ALL. I WILL GO TO THEM ALL. SHE WILL HELP ME. THE WOMAN WILL HELP ME.

We were very still, very quiet, coming across the ocean from Amsterdam to Washington, DC. We didn't even look right. We looked like sticks and were only about two feet long. They made us dormant for the December trip across the ocean.

It was very important that we make it to US soil quickly. The United States Department of Agriculture (USDA) was going to close entry of HORSE CHESTNUT TREES by January 1, 2010.

All 11 of us were required to be in quarantine for three years. You heard me right - three YEARS! It was for our own good AND for the good of other trees, especially horse chestnuts.

For months I was in Beltway, MD, with the others. We were together, but separate. I was planted, awakened out of dormancy.

Were others? I think so. After all, we were important. We were the seedlings of Mother Horse Chestnut tree.

Mother was famous. She stood outside in the Amsterdam courtyard. Anne Frank wrote about Mother. When Mother got old and sick, we were cut from her DNA as seedlings. We were planted to grow and live. Mother would be so proud as we took root with hope!

Chapter 2

All of the Saplings were headed away. I am not even sure who left first or last.

Then I was put in the back seat of a car NEXT TO ANOTHER SIBLING SAPLING. I was not alone!

Yes, for three years, quarantine was our life. My New York Sibling Sapling and I spent time together in a Bronx greenhouse. We were watered and watched and studied.

A small, rural school owned me. I was groomed for pictures, emailed to them as I went through seasons and had my checkups. I passed in flying colors. No blight in me!

I was released. Work was done to get ready for me. There would be a BIG party! I was to be the star! Children and adults, school and community, press and dignitaries were all invited. Even an original score was written by a student. It was performed at the ceremony FOR ME!

The art department students created an interactive representation of the Amsterdam hiding annex and window from which Mother could be seen. There were dancers, and flags, and, and, and! Yes! The ceremony was special.

I was planted behind the rural school. A local artist designed and oversaw everything. Eventually there would be 11 boulders around the small rural school site. One would represent each of us, each awarded seedling. A holocaust survivor came and helped.

I grew. I turned colors. I dropped leaves. I grew again. I was loved. But I never stopped wondering about my sibling saplings. I could not go. I was rooted. I was loved. Sigh.

Chapter 3

The woman had retired. She almost waited until I came out of the three year quarantine. She did not wait, but she came back a year later for my planting and celebration. She would help me. She would go. She would sit. She would write. She would take pictures. She would share. The woman would help me. Then I would know.

After the celebration, the woman even wrote an unpublished book about me, "Growing an Idea ~ Rooted in Hope June 2013." It was subtitled, "A Symbol of Anne Frank's Legacy Arrives at Southern Cayuga Central School District. " She would use the book to write more when she found my Siblings.

I am shaking my limbs! The woman found a Sibling in Sonoma, California, farthest away from me in rural Central New York. A Holocaust Memorial was made bigger to include my Sibling. The woman's older son found. She sat. She wrote this, "Visited the first of ten Sibling Saplings with older son, just a couple of hours from his home. I am surprised at how much bigger this tree has grown. Were they all the same size when arriving at the USDA in Beltway, MD? Did you grow faster in quarantine because of the weather? Where did they confine you? I am the eleventh. Special that my first visit is farthest from the small rural school sapling. I am blessed." She shared. The visit to Sonoma Sibling Sapling was November 28, 2013.

I listened. I looked. I just about dropped my leaves. I was so excited!

Chapter 4

The retired woman found another Sbling Sapling on her journey from New York to Canada to Michigan. In the Farmington Hills Holocaust Museum near Detroit, a special place was made. My Sibling was planted outside, but viewed through a window from inside, just like Mother Horse Chestnut tree.

The woman had called ahead. She was given keys to go into the courtyard! No glass obstructed her view! She could not sit, but she did take pictures. She did write. She did share. More words, dated October 4, 2015, were recorded in the book. "… Apparently you grew three to four feet this summer. You are taller than the rural school tree. The center where it stands is a touching, tearful collection of stories and artifacts. I am sitting under the six skylights - symbolic of the six million who died at the hands of their oppressors. This Sapling Project is important and I will, God willing, continue the quest."

I listened. I looked. I was happy.

Chapter 5

Can you believe it? My next Sibling Sapling was very near where we arrived stateside. The woman took a train to the US Capitol Building in Washington, DC. My Sibling had a place on the West Lawn, the Capitol seen nearby. The sign was little. The roping drooped. People just walked by. They didn't know. The woman cried. She sat on a bench. She wrote through her tears. She was happy. She was sad. She stopped people to tell them what they were walking by. They did not care.

The woman almost left. She stopped one more couple. Immediately she knew the United States was not their home. THEY WERE VISITING FROM AMSTERDAM! They knew about Mother Horse Chestnut tree. They knew about Anne. They were happy the woman stopped them or they would have walked right by! Can you imagine?

The woman took their picture with my DC sibling. Everyone smiled.

She wrote again, "Third of Saplings to visit. This one via Metro Rail ride from Springfield on the Blue line after leaving Mom and Dad at a nearby hotel. I cried when I found you - affirming how important this is. I am sitting on a bench within sight of you. I have my pictures and I have questions. You are less protected here than any site I have visited. Perhaps because there are so many cameras. You are healthy and proud with the US Capitol Building over your shoulder. I stopped people who were walking by you, ignoring you, to tell them your importance. I am here. I care. I will tell the story to children and adults alike. p.s. Just after I wrote this, I stopped a couple who had just passed the tree to inquire if they knew the significance. THEY WERE FROM AMSTERDAM! How blessed I am. Thank you, God!"

The woman shared.

I listened. I looked. I was happy.

Chapter 6

Oh my goodness! A place at the National Children's Museum in Indianapolis, Indiana, was made for another Sibling Saplings. It was planted outside in a beautiful, cared-for garden. On the inside, part of the third floor was all about Anne Frank. A one-act play showcased Otto Frank, Anne's father. He returned to the Amsterdam annex and was given back young Anne's red and white checkered diary. (The woman learned later that the diary was a gift at a 13th birthday party for Anne.) Anne wrote about Mother Horse Chestnut tree as she hid with others in the annex. Then Mother became famous. It is all there.

The woman went. She sat. She took pictures. On August 18, 2016, she shared these written words, "As always, I found you! So proud. So strong. Such an important story to tell! Staying with a travel buddy. You are bigger, fuller than any of your Siblings. Your trunk is nearing four inches in diameter and you are eight to ten feet tall. Your leaves are so unique and just beginning to spot and curl. You are healthy! You are the fourth Sapling I have visited - six more, plus the small rural school in CNY tree. Thank you for sharing the story. Thank you for giving hope.

One young girl in atrocious circumstances found hope from watching Mother out of the annex window. Now it's the children's turn, the SIBLING SAPLINGS!"

I listened. I looked. I swelled with pride. I was happy.

Chapter 7

A sad thing happened to the retired woman. Her father died. After the funeral on an unplanned trip into New York City, she agreed to go and look for my extra special Sibling Sapling! Remember? I rode in the back seat of a car for three years of quarantine with New York Sibling in that Bronx greenhouse!

Liberty Garden at the World Trade Center Memorial was to be home to my special New York Sibling Sapling. No one knew. Blank stares and shaking heads were all that met the woman. She left, not knowing she had stood just yards from the barely marked tree. Sibling had been quietly planted. A formal ceremony was planned with press for six months later. The woman would have to go back. She left without writing.

Chapter 8

Then the woman got sick. She was not finished. Oh. I get sad just thinking about it. Would I ever learn about ALL of my Sibling Saplings?

The woman never drove again. She did get stronger. She used help. She had a plan to visit the others. She could visit the six Horse Chestnut tree Saplings. She could make just three trips. She could sit in her wheelchair. She could take pictures with her phone. She could write. She could share.

The woman hadn't gone yet. She got sick first in September 2017 and then again in early March 2020.

Will she ever go? Will she ever finish the visits for me? Will I ever know? Sigh.

Chapter 9

Things change. Places change. People change. Saplings change.

The world shut down. COVID-19 brought quarantine for much of the planet. People were often alone. They were separated. They died alone and with strangers.

I knew about quarantine. My Siblings knew, or so I thought.

The now disabled woman was blessed. Life was very different, but belief came back. Technology helped.

It started with a radio interview in 2021. A new book was published with illustrations. Five others were republished with illustrations too. Each had a video book trailer on the woman's website.

The disabled woman grew stronger. Devices were accepted as part of life. She never drove again, but she could fly! She could live independently. She could ride an electric scooter. She could order groceries with her phone. She could use a computer. She could write. She could take pictures. She could share.

Chapter 10

When visiting her son in California, the woman began believing that visiting my Siblings could be completed in just two years. I was very, very happy!

The disabled woman started making plans. Three flights. Six saplings. Two years, 2023 and 2024. Details. Help. Rides.

Chapter 11

What happened next is not real. It shakes through to my roots. I bow my boughs. I shed leaves like tears. Oh, how can this be? HOW CAN THIS BE?

The woman had to tell. For one trip she only had to go back to New York City. A cruel person vandalized my planted Sibling Sapling in the Boston Commons! Sibling was dug up and taken back into quarantine. There the Boston Horse Chestnut tree died. Oh!!! It makes me SO mad. I am rooted. I am thriving. I would take Sibling's place if I could.

How can I go on knowing one of the eleven has died?

The woman whispered to me. She promised it would be okay. She promised to go and sit and write and share of the others. I promised to listen.

Chapter 12

Visiting the little Central New York school in the summer of 2023, the woman sat by me and wrote. "My, how you've grown. I am thrilled by your health. I swell with pride. This is part of my legacy. You are part of my legacy. I don't trust that I can call you a sapling anymore. You are a tree, a proud tree. Mother would be proud. "

Then I remembered. Eleven boulders surrounded me at the small school. Each one represents a Sapling. One was for me. When the 11 started, all were heading into quarantine for three years. All had homes. Now one was gone. My core tugged. I missed you, Sibling. My boughs lifted for you. You tried your best.

Chapter 13

The disabled woman had other sad news to tell. She was planning the first trip to Arkansas to visit, to sit, to write, to share. A teacher friend told the woman she did not have to go to Hope or Little Rock. In both places my Sibling Saplings DIED. They did not adjust to the climate. It just can't be true. No. NO. NOOOOOOO. IT JUST CANT BE TRUE!

SIBLINGS DO NOT DIE YOUNG! TREES ARE SUPPOSED TO THRIVE AND HAVE MANY RINGS! THE WOMAN IS SUPPOSED TO GO TO ARKANSAS!

Praying, I bargained with God. "Lord, you can do this. You can bring anything back to life. You will help the woman go and she will find my Sibling Saplings alive! I will honor you always! Yes, Lord? Yes?"

The long days will get shorter. My leaves will fall. The air will get cold. I don't want to wake up. I ache. I am sad.

The days start to get longer again. The woman reminds me that somehow I can honor my three deceased Siblings. I like that idea. Perhaps the boulders surrounding me, the rural CNY Sapling, can be tagged. Yes, that is a good way to remember.

Chapter 14

The disabled woman prepared to fulfill a goal. The woman would travel back to the city. It would be different. It would be good.

Calls were made. The woman told. She was coming to New York City. Special New York City Sibling would be found on this first trip.

A call to a new friend made an important connection. As executive director of the Anne Frank Foundation in New York City, the new friend was very much a part of Mother Horse Chestnut tree's seedlings, their distribution, and their planting. "Go to Liberty Garden," the new friend said. "It's near the World Trade Center's Reflecting Pools. The tree is healthy." New friend remembered that special connection. New friend remembered that we rode in the back seat of a car together. New friend remembered that we spent three years in quarantine in that Bronx greenhouse.

New friend told that 20 seedlings started the voyage across the ocean from Amsterdam. Nine did not survive. That is why only 11 of us were awarded from grants around the country. Thirty-six places had applied for the grant. Yes, new friend wanted to keep the connection and our story alive!

New York City bound, the disabled woman and old friend were close to the World Trade Center. Old friend was from near

Boston. Searching for Special Sibling, the woman fought back tears. When the long ramp got her to Liberty Garden, the woman scooted right past New York Sibling Sapling. Old friend shouted and called the woman back, back to my Sibling Sapling!

The woman cried. She wrote this: "Hello Sibling! You grow. You drop leaves. You look like Mother Horse Chestnut tree to me. You are a sign of hope. Here at Liberty Park World Trade Center, you thrive. Busy city noise is behind us. Do you remember our years in quarantine together? Look how we spread the news. We keep sharing hope, just like Anne believed when she gazed at Mother out the window. Be well. Feel love."

Old friend took pictures. The disabled woman talked to you, Special Sibling. How wonderful it was for all!

I listened. I looked. I cried. You were healthy like me! You were a growing young tree like me! You knew young Anne's story lived long after her short life. You were part of the legacy. We were part of Mother's legacy. We lived to tell the story!

Chapter 15

Another plan. Another year. Another month. Another day. Another place. The woman was guided to my tenth Sibling in Seattle. This second of three journeys was long. The whole way, diagonally across the country, the disabled woman flew alone. Within minutes of arrival, her older son and daughter-in-law greeted the disabled woman. They had flown in, too. It was all part of the plan.

Older son pushed the woman in her wheelchair. A new Seattle friend met the three on a cold January winter day in Washington state. It was 16°F! The woman gave the new Seattle friend the book about ME!

There in the shadow of the famed Space Needle, you, thriving Sibling Sapling, stood. The new Seattle friend was thrilled to meet someone who wanted to talk about Anne Frank and trees! She told how she had been part of writing the grant to receive the Sibling in Seattle. She knew about the three year quarantine. New Seattle friend knew that, unlike me, Sibling's three year quarantine kept Seattle Sibling Sapling right at the USDA in Beltway, MD. She knew the Seattle Department of Parks and Recreation would decide to keep you in quarantine in Seattle for yet another three years! So, in 2016 you were finally planted. You were placed in the Peace Gardens near the Space Needle.

You brought hope to the city of Seattle. You made Mother Horse Chestnut tree proud! You looked so good, even in your stark state of winter quiet. You had growing, reddish buds, promising hope, promising life, promising spring!

The woman showed you pictures of me. She told how we were connected. She came. She saw.

The woman cried as she wrote, "I see you with family and new friend. The Space Needle is right behind. I am so happy. I have tears of joy that I can be here. You are here. HOPE is HERE. Even in your winter starkness, you have buds. You are beautiful. I will share. All will know. You have blessed yet again." Son took pictures. She shared.

The woman even autographed the book about me for her new Seattle friend. Assurance was given that the woman would come back and stay connected. Finding Sibling Sapling number ten was literally in the books.

I listened. I looked. I wept.

Chapter 16

I smiled through my tears. It was all really happening. Yes, me, the rural CNY Horse Chestnut tree was seeing the dream come true. The woman, long disabled now, was helping me. Our story was being told. Anne's belief of hope in the seasons of Mother Horse Chestnut tree was growing around the country. The homework given to the woman was coming true.

You, me, all of us, had become a lifeline of hope for the disabled woman. We became her passion, her rooted lifeblood, her purpose. Sibling Saplings can do that! Trees can do that! We can do that! We have done that! Mother IS proud!

Chapter 17

In her excitement the woman called teacher friend. She shared the idea to label each of the 11 boulders. There at the CNY rural school, teacher friend recommended the idea be modified. Apparently, children play on the boulders around the tree and next to the playground. The boulders roll when pushed. Boulders have been retrieved from ditches! It is SO perfect. Children play. Children laugh. Children emulate hope.

So instead teacher friend would contact the local artist who had found the grant idea to take to teacher friend AND designed the planting/learning area for me. The local artist would have an additional sign made and added to the site to honor the original 11 awarded Horse Chesnut tree Saplings. If all goes well, the sign can be dedicated on the annual birthday celebration for Anne Frank at the rural school in CNY with me! It is a perfect plan!

Chapter 18

The woman was curious. How big had Sibling Saplings gotten that had been seen long ago?

Places responded with pictures just taken in 2023. Sonoma State University College in California sent a beautiful picture of Sibling in fall colors with the sun shining. So big! So beautiful. Comparisons were made with the pictures the woman took years ago. Health was evident. The disabled woman shared.

Response from the Holocaust Museum in Farmington Hills, Michigan, showed their tree in spring. The buds on the Horse Chestnut tree Sibling were pink and white. They looked like little Christmas trees. The beauty was breathtaking! The health of this tree, no longer a seedling nor a Sapling, was undeniable! The woman could not wait to share!

The Capital Building West Lawn tree pictures came. A friend took the photos. Perspective was difficult. All things that can grow did grow! The signage was questionable. Anne Frank was not mentioned. One wonders if the horrific storming and vandalism at the capital had anything to do with it. The woman wondered. Perhaps antisemitism caused officials there to be cautious. The woman told me and I shook my branches.

Chapter 19

Remember how I told about the woman writing in her book when she sat by Sibling Saplings? In between seeing the tenth and eleventh tree, the woman spilled and splattered coffee on the writings. Quickly she blotted the pages dry, but the stain remained. The disabled woman wrote, "Well, it makes it more real."

Chapter 20

The woman had to tell me something. It was a secret. I did not want to hear. I did not want to know. She might tell me about death again. I DID NOT WANT TO KNOW. NO MORE STAINS!

The woman assured me that it would be alright. Happy reasons were at the heart of the secret. The last Sapling, the Boise Sibling Sapling, was doing very well. The city planners were taking good care of Sibling at the Anne Frank Human Rights Memorial there. They were in communication with the woman. They shared of their deep commitment to the real fight against antisemitic violence in Boise. They were committed to keeping Sibling Sapling safe. They were committed to education.

It was then that the woman knew. She knew technology would allow her to write about Sapling. The woman would talk to people, trust them, and stay connected. The disabled woman did not have to go, but she could write and share. This third trip did not have to happen.

Share she did, "Wednesday, January 31, 2024. Dear Sibling Sapling, We have both grown. You grew into a flourishing, strong tree. I grew. A lifeblood of hope floods my veins, taking root in goodness, promising to tell. It's all here at the Boise, Idaho Anne Frank Human Rights Memorial. I write not sitting in your shadow, but with confidence that comes from seeing pictures, talking to city officials, and trusting my core. I learn the same way the small rural school tree learns. History is repeated, recorded and passed down. Mother Horse Chestnut tree could not be more proud. Thank you, Boise Sibling. Thank you."

I listened. I smiled. I knew. I had asked the woman to help me. The woman, yes, the disabled woman did just that. Everyone of my ten Sibling Saplings were found. Every story was shared.

We are not together, but we are connected. Our roots run deep. Our message is clear.

Chapter 21

Complete with stains, life can be messy. Blood can splatter. The Holocaust can happen. The Holocaust did happen. Jews were persecuted, even marched to their death in gas chambers. Jews were buried in mass graves.

Anne Frank, with family and friends, hid in that Amsterdam Annex. Anne watched Mother Horse Chestnut tree through the days and seasons and years. Despite the stained world, this young girl believed in goodness. She had hope. She saw it in Mother. She wrote.

Young Anne died in a concentration camp with Typhoid Fever. Only her father, Otto Frank, lived until freed. Otto was the one who was given back young Anne's checkered diary, the same diary she had received at a birthday party. It had been found scattered, splattered on the floor. It had been gathered to give to Otto. He would share. He did share.

Hope lives. Saplings can spread hope. The woman will help us.

Washington D.C.
6-9-16

Farmington Hills, MI
10-4-15

Indianapolis, IN
8-18-16

NEW YORK CITY, NY
10-27-23

Seattle, WA
1-13-24

Aurora, NY
6-18-13

Sonoma, CA
11-29-13

Author
MARY KAY WORTH
writes
Southern Cayuga
Central School

Aurora, NY

TUESDAY
7 18 2023

www.ingramcontent.com/pod-product-compliance
Lightning Source LLC
Chambersburg PA
CBHW031240120626
46545CB00003B/1216